MILWAUKEE
The Delaplaine
Long Weekend Guide

TABLE OF CONTENTS

Chapter 1
WHY MILWAUKEE?

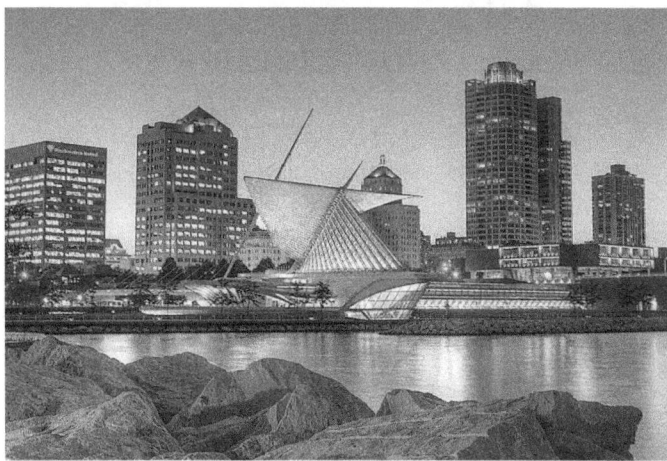

Known as "The Beer Capital of the World," Milwaukee is a lot more than beer and pretzels even though you can find more than 10 different breweries and brewpubs within the city limits.

Milwaukee, the largest city in Wisconsin, is the 30th most populous city in the United States. Visitors flock to Milwaukee every summer for the many festivals celebrating almost every ethnicity (German Fest, Irish Fest, Polish Fest) but the most famous of

MILWAUKEE
The Delaplaine
2021 Long Weekend Guide

Andrew Delaplaine

GET 3 FREE NOVELS
Like political thrillers?
See next page to download 3 great page-turners—
FREE - no strings attached.

NO BUSINESS HAS PAID A SINGLE PENNY OR GIVEN _ANYTHING_ TO BE INCLUDED IN THIS BOOK.

Senior Editors - *Renee & Sophie Delaplaine*
Senior Writer - **James Cubby**

Gramercy Park Press
New York London Paris

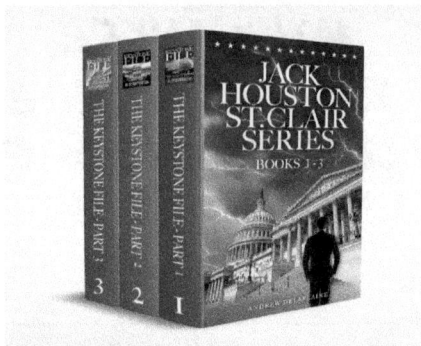

2

all is **Summerfest**, known as the "World's Largest Musical Festival."

Sports fans know Milwaukee as the home of two professional sports teams, the Milwaukee Brewers and the Milwaukee Bucks.

The **Harley-Davidson Museum**, one of Milwaukee's most popular attractions, appeals to a wide audience from hipsters to rednecks.

Whereas in Europe you have real counts and barons, here the term "beer baron" can apply to any number of families with deep roots in Milwaukee. Milwaukee's brewing history is reflected in names of local landmarks like Miller Park, Pabst Mansion, Pabst Theater, Pfister Hotel, and Schlitz Audubon Nature Center.

Milwaukee, a blue-collar town, also celebrates the workingman at the **Grohmann Museum** with the Man at Work Collection documenting the evolution of organized work over 400 years.

Milwaukee, not reflective of the "Laverne & Shirley" era, has recently revitalized with many new skyscrapers, condos, apartment buildings and lofts, most located on or near the lakefront and riverbanks. After years of declining population, common to a lot of cities in the "Rust Belt," Milwaukee has bounced back big time, seeing its population rise as young people moved into areas like Walker's Point and Bay View, for instance, helping to revitalize the entire town.

It's a really fun town, and I know you'll enjoy it.

Chapter 2
GETTING ABOUT

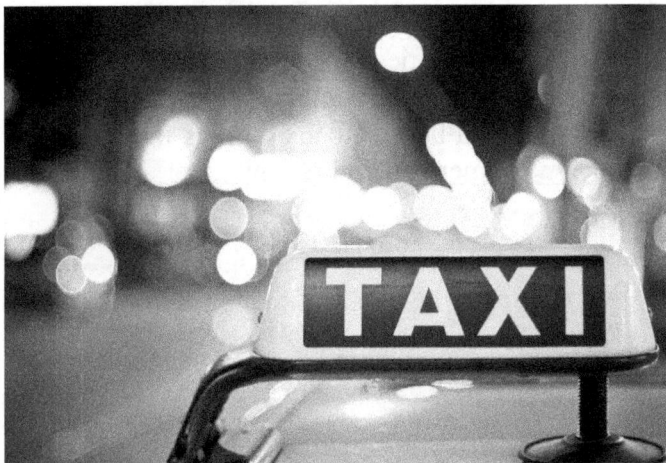

Visitors will discover that Milwaukee is an easy city to navigate as the block numbers are consistent across the city: numbered streets run north-south and most named streets run east-west. For more detailed information visit these sites:

Visit Milwaukee, 800-554-1448,
www.VisitMilwaukee.org

Travel Wisconsin, 800-432-8747,
www.TravelWisconsin.com

Airports
Timmerman Field

Milwaukee has two active airports, General Mitchell
International Airport and the smaller Timmerman
Field. Mitchell Airport, the largest airport in
Wisconsin and the 34th largest in the nation, is served
by 12 airlines making nonstop or direct flights to
approximately 90 cities. The terminal is open 24
hours a day and is just 10 minutes from downtown
Milwaukee. You'll find a bank of taxis waiting for
you. www.timmermanairport.com

Tourist Trolley

Tourists love getting around via the **Trolley Loop**, a frequent scheduled tour bus loop sponsored by local businesses, where the ride is free (or a nominal charge) and the service is seasonal.

Bus

Milwaukee's bus system, the most economical way to travel besides walking or biking, offers extensive coverage and frequent service. Many locals take advantage of the express buses called "Freeway Flyers" that provide service from park and ride lots to Downtown, Brewers games and festivals. There's also a local bus and an express bus that serves Mitchell International Airport. Most buses run from around 5 a.m. until midnight. Bus drivers only accept exact bus fare. www.ridemcts.com

Chapter 3
WHERE TO STAY

BRUMDER MANSION BED & BREAKFAST
3046 W Wisconsin Ave, Milwaukee, 414-342-9767
www.milwaukeebedbreakfast.com
NEIGHBORHOOD: Concordia
Located on the Westside, this beautiful, historic
mansion offers six guest suites complete with
fireplaces and whirlpool spas. An ideal choice for a
romantic weekend with an atmosphere of antique
elegance. This charming B&B has quite a history and
even a ghost or two. Experience their Murder

Mystery series. Amenities include: Flat screen TVs, high-def Direct TV, and free breakfast.

HAMPTON INN & SUITES MILWAUKEE DOWNTOWN
176 W Wisconsin Ave, Milwaukee, 414-271-4656
http://hamptoninn3.hilton.com/en/hotels/wisconsin/hampton-inn-and-suites-milwaukee-downtown-MKEDWHX/index.html
NEIGHBORHOOD: West Town, Downtown
Has 138 comfortable guestrooms and suites. Located downtown within walking distance of the entertainment and business district. Amenities include: Free Wi-Fi, free hot breakfast, heated-indoor pool, and Fitness Center.

HOTEL METRO
411 E Mason St, Milwaukee, 414-272-1937
www.hotelmetro.com
NEIGHBORHOOD: East Town, Downtown.
Located in downtown, this hip, eco-friendly boutique hotel offers comfortable European-style suites in a historic Art Deco building. Amenities include: 24-

hour concierge and room service, free Aveda bath
products, on-site Fitness Center with saltwater hot tub
and waterfall massage, sauna, and on-site Spa. This is
a Pet-Friendly hotel.

IRON HORSE HOTEL
500 W. Florida St, Milwaukee, 414-374-4766
www.TheIronHorseHotel.com
NEIGHBORHOOD: Walker's Point
This modern boutique hotel is set in a 100-year old
warehouse that has been beautifully transformed into
a one-of-a-kind hotel. This is the first upscale hotel
that has been geared especially for business travelers
and motorcycle enthusiasts. Amenities include: 24-
hour business center, computer station, audiovisual
equipment, pool table, free wired and wireless
internet access, 48-inch plasma TVs, and designer
toiletries. On-site restaurant and bar. On-site spa with
an impressive menu of body treatments and facials.

Located just minutes from the Harley Davidson Museum and Riverside Theater.

KNICKERBOCKER ON THE LAKE HOTEL
1028 E Juneau Ave, Milwaukee, 414-276-8500
www.knickerbockeronthelake.com
NEIGHBORHOOD: East Town.
Located on the shores of Lake Michigan, this restored Classical Revival boutique hotel offers an elegant atmosphere with 180 upscale suites and guestrooms. The Knickerbocker's grand foyer boasts original terrazzo floors, vaulted ceilings and crystal chandeliers. Amenities include: on-site parking, 24-hour Fitness Center, digital media and Wi-Fi access. The Knickerbocker features two on-site restaurants and a full-service spa and salon. Walking distance to the famous Lakefront Festivals such as Summerfest, the largest music festival in the nation.

PFISTER HOTEL
424 E. Wisconsin Ave, Milwaukee, 414-273-8222
www.ThePfisterHotel.com
NEIGHBORHOOD: East Town, Downtown.
With a reputation as Milwaukee's most famous and
luxurious hotel, the Pfister offers 307 lavishly
decorated non-smoking guest rooms and suites.
Amenities include: round-the clock personal service,
wireless high-speed internet access, indoor pool, free
use of fitness center, LCD Flat TVs, iPod/MP3
Compatible Radio/alarm, and 24-hour movies. Onsite
spa and salon, gift shop and men & women's
fashions. **Blu Bar and Lounge** on the 23rd floor
offers panoramic views, and onsite dining
opportunities include **Mason Street Grill**, The Café,
The Rouge and the Lobby Lounge. Within walking

distance to shopping, nightlife, museums, theater and top-notch dining.

MANDERLEY BED & BREAKFAST
3026 W Wells St, Milwaukee, 414-459-1886
www.bedandbreakfastmilwaukee.com
NEIGHBORHOOD: Concordia
Located on the Westside near the Bed and Breakfast district, this Queen Anne mansion offers a welcoming atmosphere reminiscent of the late1800s and it's no wonder that this house is listed on the National Register of Historic Places. Six fireplaces, intricate woodwork, and hand painted walls lend to the romantic feel of the mansion. Amenities include: Free breakfast, in-room internet/WiFi, fireplace, hot tub/whirlpool tub, and TV/VCR. Conveniently located near downtown Milwaukee and attractions.

SAINT KATE - THE ARTS HOTEL

139 E Kilbourn Av, Milwaukee, 414-276-8686
www.saintkatearts.com
NEIGHBORHOOD: East Town, Downtown.
In the heart of downtown, this hotel offers fine and comfortable accommodations. Amenities include: LCD flat panel TV, 24-hour room service, nightly turn-down service, high-speed internet and wireless service, mp3 docking station, and mini bar snack baskets. On-site Health Club. Centrally located near the scenic Milwaukee Riverwalk, theatre district, restaurants and nightlife.

SCHUSTER MANSION
3209 W Wells St, Milwaukee, 414-342-3210
www.SchusterMansion.com
NEIGHBORHOOD: Concordia
Located in the Bed and Breakfast district, this 1891
Victorian mansion offers a luxurious alternative to the
norm. Here you feel you've stepped back in time and
each room has its own charm and style. Amenities
include: free breakfast, free internet WiFi access,
TV/DVD, whirlpool, and DVD library. High tea
served daily. Conveniently located near downtown
Milwaukee and attractions like The Bradley Center
and Miller Park Stadium.

Chapter 4
WHERE TO EAT

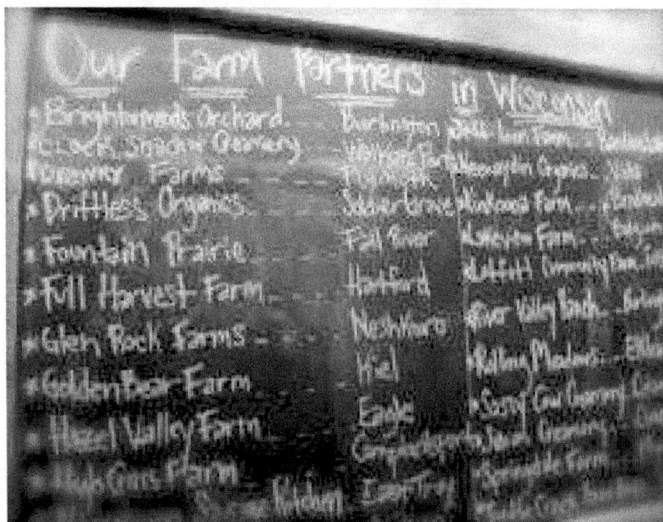

BRAISE
1101 S. 2nd St, Milwaukee, 414-212-8843
www.BraiseLocalFood.com
CUISINE: American, Tapas
DRINKS: Full Bar
SERVING: Dinner
PRICE RANGE: $$
NEIGHBORHOOD: Walker's Point

Located in a warehouse transition neighborhood, Braise is a cooking school and a restaurant. This locally sourced eatery focuses on simple and fresh ingredients, with interesting options for vegetarians. Menu favorites include: Risotto with ham and roast chicken. Great desserts. Good service. This is Milwaukee's first Community Supported Restaurant and memberships are available.

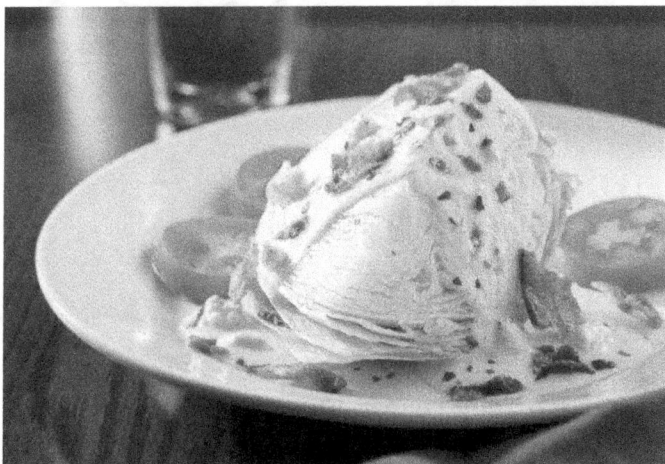

THE CAPITAL GRILLE
310 W Wisconsin Av, Milwaukee, 414-223-0600
www.thecapitalgrille.com
CUISINE: American, Steakhouses
DRINKS: Full Bar
SERVING: Lunch & Dinner
PRICE RANGE: $$$
NEIGHBORHOOD: West Town, Downtown.
The popular steakhouse chain has an outpost here.

FIVE O'CLOCK STEAKHOUSE

2416 W State St, Milwaukee, 414-342-3553
www.fiveoclocksteakhouse.com
CUISINE: Hawaiian, Steakhouses
DRINKS: Full Bar
SERVING: Dinner
PRICE RANGE: Dinner
NEIGHBORHOOD: Avenues West
Old school steakhouse that serves great food and the
portions are just as impressive as the quality. The
usual list of cuts of beef, but they're also famous for
their hickory smoked BBQ baby back rubs.

LEON'S FROZEN CUSTARD
3131 S 27th St, Milwaukee, 414-383-1784
www.leonsfrozencustard.us
CUISINE: Ice Cream & Frozen Yogurt; sandwiches
DRINKS: No Booze
SERVING: Lunch, Dinner
PRICE RANGE: $
NEIGHBORHOOD: Southgate
This place is a Milwaukee icon, dating back to 1942. Remember the TV show Happy Days"? This place is supposedly the inspiration for the drive-in Arnold's. I believe it. The frozen custard comes in flavors like strawberry, raspberry, mint, maple walnut and cinnamon, among many others. Burgers and chili dogs are also served, but if you're short on time, get the wonderful burger across the street at **Mazos** and come here for a frozen custard for dessert afterwards.

MADER'S RESTAURANT
1041 N Old World 3rd St, Milwaukee, 414-271-3377
www.madersrestaurant.com
CUISINE: German
DRINKS: Full Bar
SERVING: Lunch & Dinner
PRICE RANGE: $$$
NEIGHBORHOOD: Bronzeville, West Town
Victor Mader runs this place, which has been in business since 1902. This classic old-style German restaurant serves traditional German cuisine in a fancy, historic atmosphere. Food portions are gigantic. As you would expect of any place in Milwaukee (especially a German one), the beer selection is outstanding. Start off with some "Reuben Rolls": corned beef, sauerkraut and Swiss cheese wrapped inside a spring roll, served with crispy fried spinach and Dusseldorf mustard sauce. After that, get the Steak Oscar and Lobster mac and cheese. (Also good are the duck sliders.)

There's a lengthy list of Schnitzels. Delicious desserts include German Chocolate cake with caramel. Presidents Kennedy, Reagan and Ford have eaten here.

MAZOS HAMBURGERS
3146 S 27th St, Milwaukee, 414-671-2118
www.mazoshamburgers.com **WEBSITE DOWN**
CUISINE: Burgers
DRINKS: No Booze
SERVING: Lunch, Dinner
PRICE RANGE: $
NEIGHBORHOOD: Southgate
When I'm here, I always get the bacon cheeseburger and the homemade soup of the day. They've been serving juicy burgers here since 1934 and they don't come any better. The beef here is ground daily. Never

frozen. Shakes and malts. (And the low prices are nice.)

MILWAUKEE CHOPHOUSE
Hilton Hotel
633 N 5th St, Milwaukee, 414-226-2467
www.milwaukeechophouse.com
CUISINE: American, Seafood, Steakhouses
DRINKS: Full Bar
SERVING: Dinner
PRICE RANGE: $$$
NEIGHBORHOOD: West Town, Downtown
Located on the ground floor of the Milwaukee Hilton, this steakhouse offers a complete dining experience in a quiet, elegant atmosphere. Menu favorites include: Poblano Remoulade Crab Cakes, the signature ChopHouse Salad, and Striped Sea Bass. Impressive wine list. The steaks here are carefully prepared on an open-hearth grill and prepared with a custom blend of seasonings. They feature Scavuzzo's steaks (from Kansas City) and Breckenridge Farms pork. Fruits and vegetables come from local growers.

MO'S
720 N Plankinton Av, Milwaukee, 414-272-0720
www.mosaplaceforsteaks.com
CUISINE: Steakhouses
DRINKS: Full Bar
SERVING: Dinner
PRICE RANGE: $$$$
NEIGHBORHOOD: West Town, Downtown
One of three national locations, the others being in Houston and Indianapolis, Mo's is definitely "a place

for steaks," as they like to say. Standouts: Filet Au Poivre and the bacon-wrapped scallops. For dessert you could do worse than try The Cookie, a giant freshly baked cookie with a scoop of vanilla ice cream.

MOTOR BAR & RESTAURANT
401 W Canal St, Milwaukee, 414-287-2778
www.motorrestaurant.com
CUISINE: American, Pubs
DRINKS: Full Bar
SERVING: Lunch & Dinner
PRICE RANGE: $$
NEIGHBORHOOD: Menomonee River Valley
Comfort food like burgers, fries, sandwiches, salads and big delicious baskets of cheese curds, something of a local phenomenon created because everybody up in these parts lives and breathes cheese. Located next to the Harley-Davidson Museum, this diner-inspired restaurant also serves Pig Skins and Wood-Grilled

Sausage Cuts. They have a specialty burger every month. When I was there, it was called "Spring Fresh," and included a hand packed 8 oz. beef patty topped with feta cheese, arugula, tomatoes, red onions, lemon aioli and a black olive tapenade on rosemary focaccia. Oh, and of course, it was served with a bunch of thick-cut fries. The peach cobbler comes in a hot skillet with a large dollop of ice cream on top. God, it's good.

THE SAFE HOUSE
779 N Front St, Milwaukee, 414-271-2007
www.safe-house.com
CUISINE: American
DRINKS: Full Bar
SERVING: Lunch, Dinner & Late Night
PRICE RANGE: $$
NEIGHBORHOOD: East Town, Downtown
Hidden behind International Exports Ltd, this is an elaborate spy themed restaurant and you enter through an alley. This is a must-see if you're visiting Milwaukee. Inside there's a Spy Museum and even a few entertainers. Menu items are also themed: the "Custom Spy Burger." Video monitors allow you to watch other patrons entering and acting silly. There's even a secret exit but you must pay a quarter.

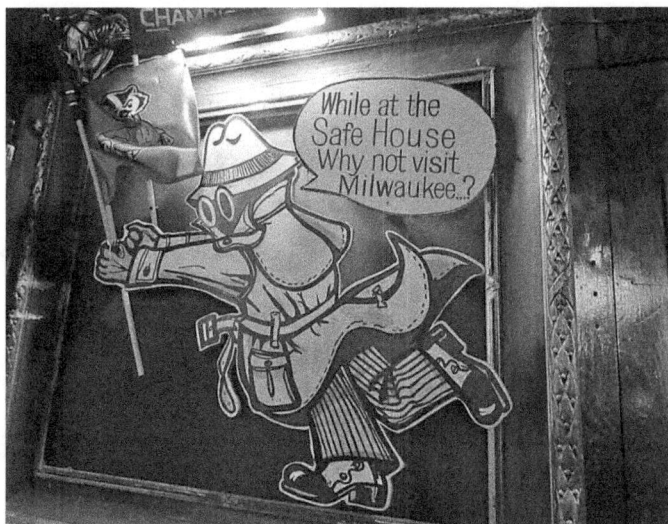

SANFORD

1547 N Jackson St, Milwaukee, 414-278-9608

www.sanfordrestaurant.com

CUISINE: American

DRINKS: Full Bar

SERVING: Dinner

PRICE RANGE: $$$$

NEIGHBORHOOD: Lower East Side

If you only have one night in Milwaukee, I'd hit this place for dinner. It's considered one of the best places in the whole Midwest. Though original owner Sandy D'Amato (who cooked for Julia Child on her 80th birthday) doesn't own it anymore (he sold it to long-time Chef de Cuisine Justin Aprahamian and his wife), it's run just the way Sandy ran it. The cuisine is described as Modern Ethnic, taking food traditions from around the world and creating modern dishes. Expect things like: Watercress soup with egg and confit potatoes; prawns and rabbit sausage with lentils; grilled pear & Roquefort tarte with onions; pumpkin soup; quail glazed with molasses. I usually don't order off the menu if I'm here during a weeknight because they have as "Surprise Tasting Menu" with wine pairings that I always get. You never know what you're getting, but it's always great.

ZAFFIRO'S PIZZA
1724 N Farwell Ave, Milwaukee, 414-289-8776
www.zaffirospizza.com
CUISINE: Pizza
DRINKS: Full Bar
SERVING: Lunch, Dinner
PRICE RANGE: $$
NEIGHBORHOOD: Lower East Side
The best pizza in town. There is such a thing as Milwaukee style pizza, notable not only for the high quality of the cheese and sauce, but for the way the round pie is cut into squares. There's a bar on one side of the room and tables on the other side sporting checkered tablecloths like the ones you used to see in old fashioned Italian restaurants. (This place has been

around since the 1950s.) If you get sausage on your
pizza, you'll know it was made by a local supplier.

Chapter 5
NIGHTLIFE

Nightlife in Milwaukee is more varied than you might think. A lot of the old former warehouses in the Third Ward have been converted into nightspots. These are right on the river. Water Street is where you'll find most bars. Also on Broadway.

The gay bars are in the Fifth Ward and Walker's Point, just across the river and a several blocks to the south.

There are about a thousand licensed taverns in Milwaukee, so you'll not have to go far to get a drink. The prices are VERY reasonable.

ART BAR

722 E Burleigh St, Milwaukee, 414-372-7880
www.artbar-riverwest.com
WEBSITE DOWN AT PRESS TIME
NEIGHBORHOOD: River West
Friendly bar with an outside seating area.

BREMEN CAFÉ

901 E Clark St, Milwaukee, 414-431-1932
www.bremencafe.com
NEIGHBORHOOD: River West
This bar sometimes has live music.

BRYANT'S COCKTAIL LOUNGE

1579 S Ninth St, Milwaukee, 414-383-2620
(Corner 9th & Lapham)
www.bryantscocktaillounge.com
NEIGHBORHOOD: Historic Mitchell Street
Don't let the unprepossessing house in which it's located put you off. inside, you'll find lots of young couples enjoying drinks served in a long bar that was caught in a time warp. Listen to the old standards by Ella Fitzgerald or Frank Sinatra or Tony Bennett while you sip an elaborate ice cream drink or an Old Fashioned. On weekends only from 8 p.m., you can go up to the second floor Velvet Lounge where you can settle in with romantic lighting with walls dressed in plush velvet, of course. The bar downstairs opens at 5. Bryant's has been here since 1938.

CACTUS CLUB

2496 S Wentworth Av, Milwaukee, 414-897-0663
www.cactusclubmilwaukee.com

NEIGHBORHOOD: Bay View
Live music venue and bar, mainly indie and punk.

FALCON BOWL
801 E Clarke St, Milwaukee, 414-264-0680
https://urbanmilwaukee.com/2016/04/06/bar-exam-falcon-bowl-a-polish-milwaukee-treasure/
NEIGHBORHOOD: River West
A legendary little bowling alley and bar. This place has a genuine old Milwaukee ambience.

HI HAT LOUNGE
1701 N Arlington Place, Milwaukee, 414-225-9330

www.hihatlounge.com
NEIGHBORHOOD: Lower East Side, East Village
Popular bar, restaurant, lounge on the corner of Brady
and Arlington. North Avenue is a few blocks north of
Brady and is a very popular bar street, especially with
the college crowd. There are a number of bars within
a few blocks of each other on North and side streets.

THE NOMAD
1401 E Brady St, Milwaukee, 414-224-8111
www.nomadworldpub.com
Small but very popular place. Has big windows
overlooking Brady Street.

PALOMINO BAR
2491 S Superior St, Milwaukee, 414-747-1007
www.palominobar.com
NEIGHBORHOOD: Bay View
Great Bay View hipster retro corner bar hangout.
Serves great fried vegan food.

WOLSKI'S TAVERN

1836 N Pulaski St, Milwaukee, 414-276-8130
www.wolskis.com
NEIGHBORHOOD: Lower East Side, East Village
Brady Street is the best place for people-watching.
It's busy, highly eclectic, and boasts lots of shops,
cafés and bars. Ignore them all and seek out this
famous neighborhood tavern in the historic district
just north of Brady. You'll see "I closed Wolski's"
bumper stickers all over town. If you only have time
to go to one bar in Milwaukee, make it this one.
There's a marvelous old Brunswick back bar inside
and plenty of beers on tap to go along with so many
friendly people that you'll feel like a local. Cheap,
too.

Chapter 6
WHAT TO SEE & DO

ALLEN-BRADLEY CO CLOCK
1201 S 2nd St, Milwaukee, 414-382-2000
No Website
NEIGHBORHOOD: Walker's Point
Underneath it sits the home of Rockwell Automation.
It is instantly recognizable from I-43 between
downtown and the south side of Milwaukee. It was
the largest four-sided clock in the world, until Saudi
Arabia built the largest in 2010, Al Bait Towers,
a.k.a. Mecca Royal Clock Hotel Tower. These clocks
are about 140 feet in diameter. Allen Bradley's are
40.2 feet. Milwaukee's clock is nicknamed the "Polish
moon."

BASILICA OF St JOSAPHAT

2333 S 6ᵗʰ St, Milwaukee, 414-645-5623
www.thebasilica.org
NEIGHBORHOOD: Lincoln Village
On the city's south side, it was built by the city's
Polish community from the dismantled materials of
the Old Chicago Customs House and Post Office.
Each block was carefully measured and numbered for

a best fit in the new design so that hardly any stone was re-cut or went to waste. In the end, even the original ornamental bronze railings, lighting fixtures, and doorknobs of the customs house were used for furnishings. Opulently decorated and designed, it is perhaps one of the finest examples of the so called "Polish Cathedral" style of church architecture in North America. There are weekly tours on Sunday after the 10 a.m. mass.

BETTY BRINN CHILDREN'S MUSEUM
929 E Wisconsin Av, Milwaukee, 414-390-KIDS (5437)
www.bbcmkids.org
NEIGHBORHOOD: East Town, Downtown
Large children's museum connected to the MAM via a pedestrian bridge.

CHARLES ALLIS ART MUSEUM
1801 N Prospect Av, Milwaukee, 414-278-8295
www.cavtmuseums.org
NEIGHBORHOOD: Lower East Side
19th Century French and American art, along with
Chinese and Japanese porcelains, Renaissance

bronzes, and antique furnishings. The collection is housed in a Tudor-style mansion that was designed with the intention of turning it into a museum.

CITY HALL
200 E Wells St, Milwaukee, 414-286-2150
www.city.milwaukee.gov
NEIGHBORHOOD: East Town, Downtown
It was the possibly city's most important landmark before the completion of the Calatrava addition to the museum. The architecture is heavily German influenced, and symbolizes Milwaukee's large German immigrant population at the turn of the century.

DISCOVERY WORLD
Pier Wisconsin, 500 N Harbor Drive, Milwaukee, 414-765-9966
www.discoveryworld.org
NEIGHBORHOOD: East Town, Downtown

Features in depth interactive exhibits about the Great Lakes and local natural science.

THE DOMES
MITCHELL PARK HORTICULTURAL CONSERVATORY
524 S Layton Blvd, Milwaukee, 414-257-5600
http://county.milwaukee.gov/MitchellParkConserva1 0116.htm
NEIGHBORHOOD: Mitchell Park
One of the city's most recognizable landmarks. The three huge glass domes serve as the city's horticultural gardens, and house a desert habitat, rainforest, and varying themed exhibits.

DOWNER THEATRE
2589 N Downer Ave, Milwaukee, 414-962-3120
NEIGHBORHOOD: Upper Eastside
www.landmarktheatres.com

This is one gorgeous theatre, so if there's something playing you want to see, by all means take the time to buy a ticket and go inside. It opened in 1915 as one of the finest and most modern equipped motion picture houses in a residential district in the country, making it the prototype for "neighborhood" theatres at the time. It cost nearly $65,000 to build and boasted a seating capacity of 1,200. Music being an important accessory to the motion picture back then, the Downer had not only a Weickhardt pipe organ, but an orchestra as well. Had a big facelift in 1990 when it was split into a 2-screen cinema.

HARLEY-DAVIDSON MUSEUM
400 W Canal St, Milwaukee, 877-436-8738
www.h-dmuseum.com
NEIGHBORHOOD: Menomonee River Valley
Walk through a variety of exhibits that tell the stories of the extraordinary people, products, history and culture of Harley-Davidson. In addition to the

fantastic motorcycle collection, stories are told through a variety of media: photographs, videos, apparel, rare documents and other fascinating artifacts. Peek into a portion of the Archives, never before open to the public, and home base to more than 450 motorcycles, and hundreds of thousands of artifacts that the Archives team can pull from for Museum exhibits. Admission fee.

HOAN BRIDGE
I-794. The Hoan Bridge is one of the most recognizable Milwaukee landmarks. It is a tied arch bridge suspended over the port of Milwaukee on the Milwaukee River. It's part of I-794 that leads into downtown.

MILWAUKEE ART MUSEUM
700 N Art Museum Drive, Milwaukee, 414-224-3200
www.mam.org
NEIGHBORHOOD: East Town, Downtown
The addition designed by Santiago Calatrava is one of Milwaukee's most recognizable landmarks, and the bird-like wings of the building's Quadracci Pavilion open and close several times each day, depending on the weather. These "wings" are wider than those on a Boeing 747. It takes about 4 minutes for these wings to fully deploy, and the sight is pretty amazing. I'd never seen anything quite like it. It's rather like watching some strange silver bird preparing to lift off.

But forget about the wings for a minute. This is an art museum, and inside you'll discover some 25,000 works from artists such as Audubon, Picasso, Georgia O'Keeffe, Ernst Ludwig Kirchner, Richard

Diebenkorn and Joan Miró. Exhibitions change constantly, so there's always something new and fresh going on.

There's a pretty good café inside, too, called **Café Calatrava**, with a very tasty seasonal menu. And it has great views as well. It's not stuck in some remote corner of the building, as are so many other museum cafés.

The **War Memorial**, to which the museum is connected, was designed by the architect Eero Saarinen. Modest admission fees apply, but it's free the first Thursday of every month.

MILWAUKEE COUNTY HISTORICAL SOCIETY
910 N Old World 3rd St, Milwaukee, 414-273-8288
www.milwaukeehistory.net
Right off **Marquette Park** you'll find the county historical museum. Among the historic homes they

oversee is **Trimborn Farm**, with old buildings dating back to the 19th Century when Werner Trimborn first established a farm to produce limes.

MILWAUKEE COUNTY ZOO
10001 W Bluemound Rd, Milwaukee, 414-771-3040
www.milwaukeezoo.org
NEIGHBORHOOD: Wauwatosa
One of the best zoos in the U.S., this one features 2,500 animals representing 300 species on 200 acres. Besides animal showcases, the zoo also has train tours, sea lion shows and a dairy farm. Check with zoo schedules for fun special events like sleepovers at the zoo or trick-or-treating at the zoo on Halloween.

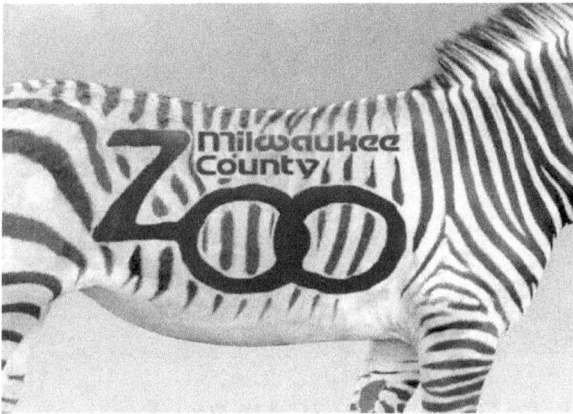

MILWAUKEE FOOD TOURS
414-255-0534
www.milwaukeefoodtours.com
This is one of the best things to do if you have the time. Taking one of these will give you a real sense of the city. They have specific tours for walking and

others involving transport by bus. On all the tours, the guides point out architectural highlights, cultural hotspots, and great restaurants and shops while sampling flavors from restaurants along the way. Choose among tours like the Brady Street Food Tour, Historic Third Ward Food Tour, Old World 3rd Street Food Tour, Bloody Mary Brunch Tour, Bay View Bloodies & Beers, Milwaukee Pizza Tour, Churches & Chocolates Tour, and several others.

MILWAUKEE PUBLIC MARKET

400 N Water St, Milwaukee, 414-336-1111
www.MilwaukeePublicMarket.com
NEIGHBORHOOD: Historic Third Ward
Sandwiches, soups, salads and seafood in a causal atmosphere. Menu prices vary from vendor to vendor, but everything's pretty reasonable. Specialty restaurants offer a wide variety of cuisines, vendors

have everything from flowers to wines to sausages, breads, freshly made cheese. Did you know that Wisconsin has more cheese makers than any other state? This market has been around for 100 years, so it's a must on your visit.

MILWAUKEE PUBLIC MUSEUM
800 W Wells St, Milwaukee, 414-278-2728
www.mpm.edu
NEIGHBORHOOD: West Town, Downtown.
On downtown's west side, it's excellent for children and adults alike, containing exhibits on numerous topics including large historical dioramas, an IMAX theater, and the largest planetarium in the state. Well-known permanent exhibits include a "Butterflies Alive" garden and the Streets of Old Milwaukee which feature the world's oldest continually functioning gas streetlight system. Admission fees.

PABST BREWERY COMPLEX
710 North Plankinton Ave, Milwaukee, 414-274-2400
www.thebrewerymke.com
The former brewery sits on the northeast side of downtown, adjacent to the Milwaukee County Courthouse and overlooking I-43. It contains many wonderful "old world" style buildings. Though the brewery is no longer in operation it still remains an icon of the city. It is currently under renovation and is being re-developed for condos, offices, and restaurants.

PABST MANSION
2000 W Wisconsin Av, Milwaukee, 414-931-0808
www.pabstmansion.com
This "Flemish Renaissance Revival" mansion built by
Captain Frederick Pabst, world famous beer baron,
accomplished sea captain, real estate developer,
philanthropist and patron of the arts, was completed
in 1892. From the day the house was inhabited, it was
considered the jewel of Milwaukee's famous avenue
of mansions called Grand Avenue and represented the
epitome of America's Gilded Age splendor in
Milwaukee. Pabst had 3,328 bottles of wine in the
cellar of this house in 1904. It has 37 rooms lavishly
decorated. The Pabsts didn't keep it long, selling it in
1908 when it became part of the archdiocese. By
1975, it was sold to become the museum it is today.
Admission fee.

VILLA TERRACE DECORATIVE ARTS
MUSEUM
2220 N Terrace Av, Milwaukee, 414-271-3656

www.villaterracemuseum.org
NEIGHBORHOOD: East Side
Fine and decorative arts from the 15th to 18th centuries. The museum is located in an Italian Renaissance-style villa built in 1923. Don't miss the Renaissance Garden in back. Admission fee.

WATER STREET BREWERY

1101 N Water St, Milwaukee, 414-272-1195
www.waterstreetbrewery.com
NEIGHBORHOOD: East Town
Located on Milwaukee's infamous Water Street, it is both a brew-pub/restaurant, but what you want to see here is the Water Street Brewery Beer Memorabilia collection that consists of one-of-a-kind beer and brewing artifacts, many of which are featured in "The World of Beer Memorabilia" book. This extensive collection is on display here.

Included are: 50,000 cans (6,000 arranged and featured in 25 impressive wood framed displays); 1,100 beer tap knobs and handles; 2,300 coasters; 825 bottle and can openers; 10 original Wisconsin Brewery lithographs; 200 server trays; 25 exterior corner signs; 450 large and miniature bottles; 50 neon signs; and many chalk figures, pictures, signs and wooden crates.

Chapter 7
BREWERIES

BEST PLACE AT THE HISTORIC PABST BREWERY
901 W Juneau Ave, Milwaukee, 414-630-1609
www.bestplacemilwaukee.com
The brewery itself has been gone for years, but the building remains one of the best places to visit. Tours are Monday, Wednesday and Friday at 2 and 4. No reservations needed. Admission fee. (And you get a 16 oz. Pabst or Schlitz while you're here.)
Gift Shop is open Wednesday-Monday 11:30 to 6.

DELAFIELD BREWHAUS
3832 Hillside Drive, Delafield, 262-646-7821
www.delafield-brewhaus.com

Microbrewery and restaurant, located 20 mi west of Milwaukee.

LAKEFRONT BREWERY

1872 N Commerce St, Milwaukee, 414-372-8800
www.lakefrontbrewery.com
NEIGHBORHOOD: Beerline B, Brewers' Hill
Yes, they've been brewing beer for a long time in Milwaukee, but this place is a sign of the future, and curiously enough, because it has reverted to the past. Small breweries are the thing now, not the corporate behemoths that have gobbled up big names. (When was the last time you had a Miller? Or a Coors? Everybody drinks craft beers now.) It's along the river in what used to be a power station and at the bottom of Brewers' Hill. If you only have time for one brewery tour, take this one, not the ones offered by Pabst or Miller. When you take the tour here, you pay $7 but look what you get: a pint beer glass, the

tour, coupons to taste up to 4 Lakefront brews, a coupon good for a beer at places in town that sell Lakefront products. Unlike other brewery tours, which give you a beer at the end of the tour, here they give it to you first! Love that. In the big hall with brick walls there's a very busy Friday night fish fry that you'll love if you're in town on a Friday.

MILLER-COORS LLC
4251 W State St, Milwaukee, 414-931-3880
www.millercoors.com
NEIGHBORHOOD: Miller Valley
This is the "other tour," and it's interesting, just not as much fun. The tours are very informative and start at their visitors' center. Most of the tour focuses on the Miller part of the operation, starting with a video that shows you all the famous Miller commercials. Then you get to go to the original brewery (this part is fun). When it's over you get to taste their beer. (Ugh! Bring a barf bag.)

MILWAUKEE ALE HOUSE
233 N Water St, Milwaukee, 414-276-2337
www.ale-house.com
NEIGHBORHOOD: Historic Third Ward
This is a brew-pub/restaurant founded by local home brewers in 1997. Has live music, fresh beer and great food. Located in a brick and timber warehouse building downtown in the historic Third Ward, they offer indoor and outdoor dining, six or more hand crafted beers, lunch and dinner everyday with late night food on the weekends.

MILWAUKEE BREWING COMPANY

1128 N. 9th St, Milwaukee, 414-226-2337
www.mkebrewing.com
NEIGHBORHOOD: Walker's Point
They give you a beer when you come in that you
carry around with you during the tour. That's nice.
Admission fee.

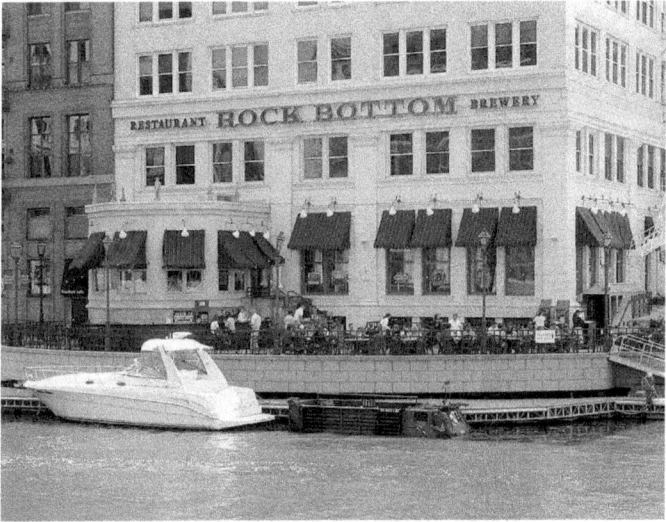

ROCK BOTTOM BREWERY

740 N Plankinton Av, Milwaukee, 414-276-3030
www.rockbottom.com/milwaukee
NEIGHBORHOOD: West Town, Downtown
This company is actually based in Colorado, but they
act like locals. They couldn't resist opening a
location in this beer town. Milwaukee River Walk.
Full menu is served: burgers, sandwiches, pizzas.

SPRECHER BREWING COMPANY

701 W Glendale Av, Milwaukee, 414-964-7837
www.sprecherbrewery.com
NEIGHBORHOOD: Grover Heights

This is a well-respected local brewery on the North Side. Known for making the largest variety of beers of any local brewery. They also offer tours, tastings included. They also make sodas, including root beer, so kids will enjoy the tour as well. You'll see their root beer sold all over town.

HONEY LAGER LIGHT
Light barley malt, clover honey and whole hops, combined to give this beer a crisp, clean flavor.
5 Tickets

IRISH STOUT
Robust hearty black Irish ale. Use of roasted barley produces coffee and dark chocolate flavors.
5 Tickets

TRINITY IRISH AMBER
Imported malt and fresh hops combine to produce a malty amber beer with a rich caramel flavor.
5 Tickets

WATER STREET BREWERY

1101 N Water St, Milwaukee, 414-272-1195
www.waterstreetbrewery.com
NEIGHBORHOOD: East Town

Located on Milwaukee's infamous Water Street, it is both a brew-pub/restaurant, but what you want to see here is the Water Street Brewery Beer Memorabilia collection that consists of one-of-a-kind beer and brewing artifacts, many of which are featured in "The World of Beer Memorabilia" book. This extensive collection is on display here.

Included are: 50,000 cans (6,000 arranged and featured in 25 impressive wood framed displays); 1,100 beer tap knobs and handles; 2,300 coasters; 825 bottle and can openers; 10 original Wisconsin Brewery lithographs; 200 server trays; 25 exterior corner signs; 450 large and miniature bottles; 50 neon signs; and many chalk figures, pictures, signs and wooden crates. On the menu they have burgers, pizza, a wide range of appetizers, sandwiches, salads, plenty of good basic food.

Chapter 8
SHOPPING & SERVICES

CLOCK SHADOW CREAMERY
138 West Bruce St, Milwaukee, 414-273-9711
www.clockshadowcreamery.com
NEIGHBORHOOD: Walker's Point
Wisconsin is the "Cheese State," right? You'd think a place so famous for its cheeses would have more cheesemongers visible, but this is the only cheese making operation in town. Lucky for you, they have tours (that last about a half-hour) and for a few bucks—they'll teach you all about the history of

cheese making and you get to sample some of their fresh cheeses, which include Quark, Chevre, Cheddar, Cheddar Curds and Mexican style cheeses. Schedule a tour on their web site, as a reservation is required.

THE EDELWEISS-CRUISE DINING VESSEL I & II

205 W Highland Av, Suite 204, Milwaukee, 414-276-7447
www.edelweissboats.com
CUISINE: American, Seafood
DRINKS: Full Bar
SERVING: Lunch & Dinner
PRICE RANGE: $$$
NEIGHBORHOOD: West Town
Elegant dinner cruises, as well as late night party cruises on the Milwaukee River, departing from the 3rd St and Highland intersection.

GLORIOSO'S ITALIAN MARKET

1011 E. Brady St., Milwaukee, 414-272-0540

www.gloriosos.com

Just a great spot to browse through. Fresh handmade sausages, mouthwatering deli creations and piping hot pizza are just a few of their specialties. Aisle after aisle of cheese, wine and pasta, olive oils, fresh and frozen pastas, bakery creations, olives, imported meats and delectable sandwiches, along with pastries, cookies, and gelato. Glorioso's has been tantalizing the public's taste buds with Mediterranean treats for over 6 decades. Upon stepping over the threshold, you can see that, four generations later, this is one store that has kept its old world charm. As you walk through the store, you will see family photos scattered throughout. If you stay long enough, you're bound to run into Joe, Ted or Eddie, the founding brothers, ready to fill you in on the history behind each photograph: from pictures when they got out of the service in WWII, to the first truck they bought for the store, to the TV commercials that feature cameos of two more family members.

MILWAUKEE BOAT LINE
101 W Michigan St, Milwaukee, 414-294-9450
www.mkeboat.com
NEIGHBORHOOD: West Town, Downtown
They have frequent cruises (with guides pointing out the sights) during the summer aboard "Vista King." You'll go along the Milwaukee River, the Harbor and Lake Michigan. Daily at noon, 2 and 4. In addition to their Historical Cruises they offer Happy Hour Cruises Tues-Sat and Concert Cruises every Friday.

PURPLE DOOR ICE CREAM
205 S 2nd St, Milwaukee, 414-988-2521
www.purpledooricecream.com
NEIGHBORHOOD: Walker's Point

Everything made in this nice little ice cream store comes from local suppliers, like the ice cream with absinthe. The absinthe comes from the Great Lakes Distillery not too far away. Besides all the usual flavors you'd expect, there are some unusual ones like raspberry green tea, salted caramel, whiskey, basil, blueberry buttermilk, among many others.

RENAISSANCE BOOKS

5300 S Howell Ave, Holler Park, 414-747-4526
NEIGHBORHOOD: Airport
https://renaissancebooksto.wixsite.com/renbookssout
hridge
A much, much smaller reincarnation of Renaissance Books, which was a legendary used bookstore in a warehouse on Plankinton Avenue that had 5 floors filled with a half-million used books. The place was dingy, many of the aisles were blocked with boxes of used books, half the windows were boarded up, and eventually the city shut it down due to "structural concerns." This is a branch of that store right in the airport. If you have to spend time at the airport, definitely spend time here. Probably the best airport book store in the country.

RUSH-MOR LIMITED MUSIC & VIDEO

2635 S Kinnickinnic Av, Milwaukee, 414-481-6040
www.rushmor.com
NEIGHBORHOOD: Bay View
One of the best remaining record stores in the city, located in Bay View. The folks here know their stuff and know what's going on in Milwaukee, as well.

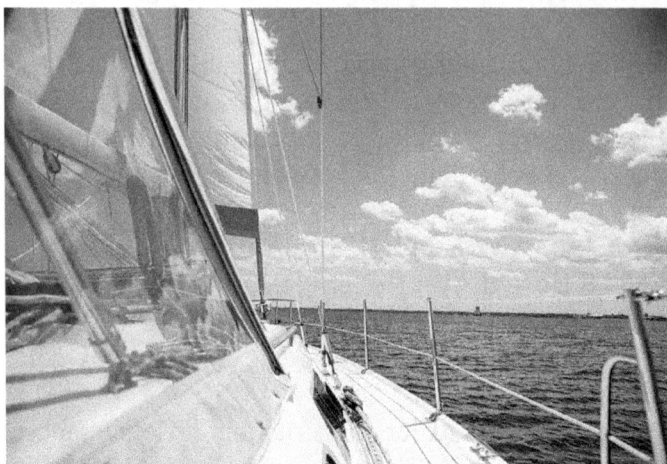

SEA DOG SAILING
McKinley Marina Center, 1750 N Lincoln Memorial
Dr, Milwaukee, 414-687-3203
www.seadogsailingmilwaukee.com
Sailing trips out of McKinley Marina.

THE SHOPS OF GRAND AVENUE
275 W Wisconsin Av, Milwaukee, 414-224-0655
www.grandavenueshops.com
NEIGHBORHOOD: West Town, Downtown
This Downtown mall is worth a visit. It features and
eclectic array of shops that sell clothing and handy
trinkets that easily fit in your luggage. There is also
plenty of Milwaukee-related stuff for sale, especially
at **Brew City**.

SKY HIGH SKATEBOARDSHOP & GALLERY
2501 S Howell Av, Milwaukee, 414-483-2585
www.skyhighskateboardshop.com
NEIGHBORHOOD: Bay View
A skate shop in Bay View with a changing selection
of Milwaukee-related gear and attire.

SPARROW COLLECTIVE
2224 S Kinnickinnic Av, Milwaukee, 414-747-9229
www.sparrowcollective.com/
NEIGHBORHOOD: Bay View
Formerly Fasten Collective offered local designers an
outlet for their work, now it's been made over and is
called Sparrow Collective, but it still sells Milwaukee
and Midwest made jewelry and clothing.

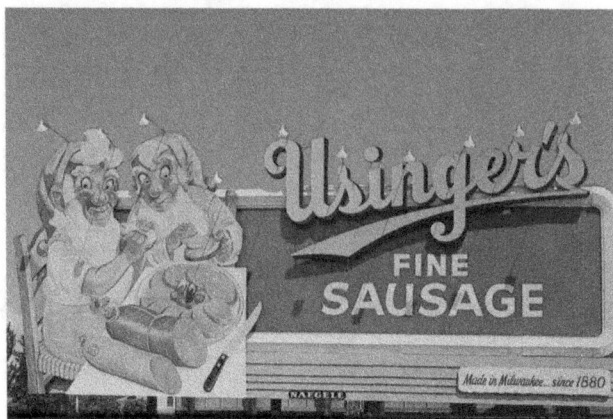

Digital Image © 2006 University of Wisconsin-Milwaukee Libraries

USINGER'S

1030 N Old World Third St, Milwaukee, 414-276-9100

www.usinger.com

NEIGHORHOOD: Westown

Get ready for a real treat when you visit the oldest sausage store in Milwaukee. It all started in 1880 when Frederick Usinger bought out the owner of the store where he was working. He'd come from Germany just a few years ago where he'd apprenticed as a "wurstmacher" (sausage maker). You'll find their products served at restaurants all over Milwaukee, but it's fun to visit the store with its clerks who have the stern attitude of a seasoned bartender. Historic photos decorate the staircases, the store, even the factory itself. From bratwurst to beerwurst, you'll find over 70 varieties of sausages sold here.

INDEX

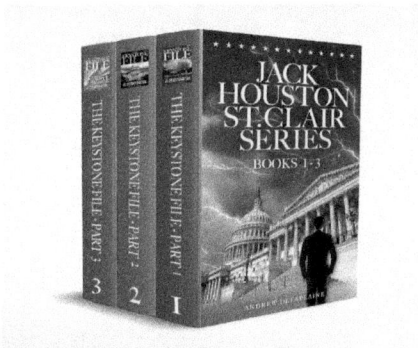

WANT 3 **FREE** THRILLERS?

Why, of course you do!

If you like these writers--

Vince Flynn, Brad Thor, Tom Clancy, James Patterson,
David Baldacci, John Grisham, Brad Meltzer, Daniel Silva,
Don DeLillo

If you like these TV series –

House of Cards, Scandal, West Wing, The Good Wife,

You'll love the **unputdownable** series about
Jack Houston St. Clair, with political intrigue, romance,
and loads of action and suspense.

Madam Secretary, Designated Survivor

Besides writing travel books, I've written political thrillers
for many years that have delighted hundreds of thousands
of readers. I want to introduce you to my work!
Send me an email and I'll send you a link where you can
download the first 3 books in my bestselling series,
absolutely FREE.

Mention **this book** when you email me.

andrewdelaplaine@mac.com